POETRY, LANGUAGE
OF THE SOUL,
VOLUME I.

Maxwanette A Poetess aka Maxine A. Moncrieffe

Published by CYBER CLERICAL ASSOCIATES

Kingston, NY 12401

www.cyberclericalassociates.com

Edited by: William Tyrone Murphy – Bronx, NY
Cover Design by: Maxwanette A Poetess aka Maxine
A. Moncrieffe Kingston, NY

First published 2020 {PLOTS LLC)
Second printing 2024

Manufactured in the United States

ISBN: 9798675487363

*NOTE: This book is not for minors, sensitive people,
the faint-hearted, or those in denial.*

DEDICATION

I would like to give my first dedication and thanks, to The Most High, The Ancestors, and My #1, My Mom, Hyacinth Williams-Moncrieffe (author & publisher of a book of poetry called "The Unlimited Mind," 1st Edition 1983, 2 Print 2024) – Rest In Love Mommy; she gave homework that drove my siblings crazy, lol! But my Mother was a firm believer and enforcer at learning begins, remains, maintains, and continues at home. Look where all those weekly vocabulary words and consistent reading have gotten me. Thank you, MaMa (Mommy). To my oldest Sister, Denise Bryan - for always putting up with me – til this day, to *William Tyrone Murphy – for having my back, no matter what, and always being there for me – "We got this Ty-Ty!" I also would like to thank a dear friend that transcended, Sister Nakato Lewis. She told me to make sure to share my poetry because the world needs it.

To my favorite teachers of Public School 316 (Elijah G. Stroud Elementary) in Brooklyn, NY; Ms. Bishop – you ran a tight ship, but it was worth every wave, To Mr. Jenkins – for being the first "Black," principal and man of intellect and strength in my life, To my 1st-grade teacher Ms. Wiener – amazed by my mind and questions, To Ms. Aldamatto (may be incorrectly spelled) – who made embracing my Jamaican culture and others, a fun thing, and to the one teacher that remains in heart...Mr. Warsaw – he was in charge of the school's bookroom...I had gotten in trouble with the principal, for stealing. However, they were not sure how to punish me, for I was stealing books, hiding away in the classroom closet, reading while others were at recess. So, I was punished, but the punishment was to write a 500-word essay about why stealing was wrong, I even voluntarily included an apology, and Mr. Warhsaw took me to the bookroom, opened it, and we went in. Oh, it was small in hindsight, but I was in 3rd grade, so the room was huge. Inside were wall-to-wall books!!! I was confused. What new torture was this going to be? But all I could do was stand in the center of the room and look around in awe. Then Mr. Warsaw told me that not only could I come and read any book I wanted in there, but I was also free to take as many as I wanted home! I cried tears of shock and joy and hugged him. I remember gently touching the tops and spines of the books, as I saw copies of Huckleberry Finn, Tom Sawyer, Paul Bunyan, Pippi Longstocking, Aesop's Fables, and so many more. I felt faint & giddy all at once. The days I spent there, reading and touching the books, smelling them...old books, new books, semi-used books...all had their own significant whiff off of the pages. They told a story all of their own. Mr. Warsaw was the gatekeeper to book heaven. I will ALWAYS love and remember him.

A special dedication to Mr. William (Bill) Howard. He was close to my mother and employed at the Grand Army Plaza, in Brooklyn, New York. He gave me access, to read books, that many would NEVER see, nor know their existence. He gave me a portal, to a knowledge that I will forever treasure. To Brother Louis Reyes Rivera, the editor of my mother's book, an activist, humanitarian, and dynamic poet – he showed me how to stand within my own strength of words and poetry. He let me know, that poetry had a voice!

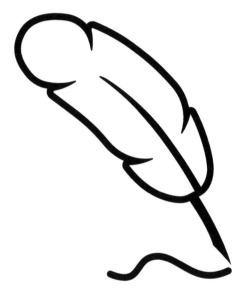

"Poetry, the language in which my Soul speaks."
~Maxwanette A Poetess

TABLE OF CONTENTS

TABLE OF CONTENTS

TABLE OF CONTENTS

FOREWORD

"Firstly, I would like to take a moment to thank everyone who has encouraged me to get my book published. My families (biological, fellow poets, & friends), have been so supportive in helping this book come to fruition."

Maxwanette wrote her 1st poem at the age of 5. It was a Haiku. Her mother was so tickled by it, that she started writing one or two every chance that she got. It drove her mother crazy, lol, but she loved it. Maxwanette's Mother, Hyacinth W.M. was the first poet she knew. She amazed her at her recitals. The way she spoke and her words captivating the audience and her voice filled with such POWER! Maxwanette knew then, that not only was her Mother amazing, she wanted to be able to reach, to connect with others with her words. With the feelings and emotions that were expressed, Maxwanette found her niche.

Being shy and an introvert, Maxwanette found it difficult to associate with others. But poetry gave her a voice. It also gave her the confidence to not only express how to feel & think, but

it is a window to the world, through this poetesses' eyes & Soul. Maxwanette stated "I have learned that poetry has a language, all of its own."

Poetry, Language Of The Soul, is like peeking through the window, yet once you peer in, you feel fully immersed into the World of Poetry. This book of poetry has a few stages; Family, Love, Heartache, Inspiration, Creativity, Livity, Resources (because we do not have all the answers & sometimes, we need more help), & Acknowledgements. It is also the 1st book in the P.L.O.T.S. Series. Volume II. is upcoming.

I thank you for being here with me, and through these stages, there follows a myriad of emotions & thoughts. I encourage the reader to have an

open mind, heart, & body, as Poetry, Language Of The Soul touches you.

~Denise C. Bryan

LOVE

I LOVE YOU

Flowing together, as the rhythmic beats of our hearts,

Play a melody, that only we can hear.

Flooding the waters of life,

As we cascade onto love's embankment.

Familiar connections, piecing the puzzles of existence,

Into a jigsaw of emotions and energies.

Causing other structures to question their reality,

As they pale in comparison to the creation & blending of our being...

"I LOVE YOU."

Sometimes, people really are unaware of the effect they have on your life. Real & true love is a powerful force. There is no other like it in its existence.

I LOVE, LOVE

I Love, Love

Simply because

of the feelings that it brings.

It lacks fear, has no cares,

And exists,

without the need of overstanding.

Lol, yes, I Love, Love!

This emotional cause,

that we use to express & give meaning to its existence.

that we use to express & give meaning to its existence.

"Muah!!!"

Lol! Oh, you lover you!

KISS *MY LIPS*

Lusciously designed, to embrace,
To taste,
The sweetness of you.

Soothingly caressing, help in undressing,
The nakedness,
Sensitive to the softness of your flesh.

Close your eyes, as I pucker on your thighs,
Darting of my tongue,
Salivating over the one, that is a delight to the pallet.

Taking you to a place, lacking of space,
For doubt, of delectable

intentions...
Oooh baby, "Kiss My Lips."

* Inspired, by the power of a kiss.

I LOVE, LOVE

I Love, Love

Simply because

of the feelings that it brings.

It lacks fear, has no cares,

And exists,

without the need of overstanding.

Lol, yes, I Love, Love!

This emotional cause,

that we use to express & give meaning to its existence.

"Muah!!!"

Lol! Oh, you lover you!

"Muah!!!"

Lol! Oh, you lover you!

BECAUSE I LOVE YOU

I had to express, how I felt.
It mattered not the cards that we're dealt.
Emotions & feelings simply do what they do.
I held this love for you, so deep within my core,
That I was no longer thinking, I was just feeling...
And wondering why I felt so trapped.

Never wanting to reveal,
emotions that made me feel,
Like no one else could ever overstand
the depth of my Soul as it wept.

Letting you know that I care,

Lol! But you've always known...

You simply weren't reciprocating &
the complication became me.
See, I feared love, I hated love,
I could not overstand the dayum thing!
But I started with me, loving all of my
being & it is a Joy that's everlasting.

So, telling you how I feel,
turned into a two-way deal,
And I released you from within my Soul,
allowing it to be healed.

Sending loves energy, back to its rightful place...

It allowed me to be free,
Because I Love You

**Inspired by what was thought to be lost loves.
Instead, it brought full circle, that Love is never lost.*

*By expressing how much I really loved someone,
allowed me to be free. I was bound to silence by my
true feelings, due to residual pains and from whatever
pain they caused, put me through or what I allowed.*

*It is okay to love people who cannot or do not love you
in return. Many simply do not know what real love is,
how to love others and even lack the love of
themselves. Sitting around in one-sided love
relationships (intimate or not) are draining and not
wise. One can lose their sense of self and so much
more, in these types of situations. Instead, I found it
best to re-examine self and why I allowed myself to
remain in such a negative space.*

*Love must start from within & with self, first.
"Real Love" exists on its own merit and embraces
those that represent it.*

*"Don't expect Love, Simply Be Love &
SPREAD IT AS FAR AS YOU CAN!"
It will always come back to you.*

I FEEL YOU

I feel you, even when you're not there.
I smell you, taste you...raising my body-hairs.

At times, the rhythm of our hearts,
cannot be undone.
Beating in unison as they become one.

Do you hear my Soul's reply?
It responds to your Morse-Coded calls.
Our telepathic Love, demolishing walls.

"Baby, I Feel You."

*Inspired by Loves' raw connections

I HEARD YOUR VOICE

It was plain and distinct.
Rich and deep.
Rumbling, like the roar in the deepest part of the
jungle.
Even though I've heard it,
so many times, before...
This time, it spoke a language, that caused my soul
to take heed.
"I Heard Your Voice."
Thousands of miles away.
Almost as if we were in two different worlds.
Through time and distance. Loud and clear.
My eyes lit up,
Blood rushed to my cheeks.

Causing a smile that illuminated my entire being.
Giggles burst forth,
As the child within,
Stuck her head out to play.
The comforting growl, of a deep and long connection,
That has ridden the skirt-tails of time.
Reaching to grab hold, of a love that will not die...
"I Heard Your Voice.

HOW LOVE IS MEANT TO BE

Reaching from a faraway place,
He calmed my soul, with the smile on his face.
Soothing away my tears,
He helped me to face my fears.
Showing me the Queen within self,
That I had forgotten, divinely saturated in grace.
He cared less of the scars on my skin
Only focusing on the condition that my heart and
soul were in.
Without shame nor care, I fell deeply in love with
him.
Fighting against him for a time,

It was difficult for my mind,
To accept the reality of the love he had shared
from within.
He stands up strong, bracing me along, our
journey,
Blending us as one, in life and for eternity.
Returned to each other, from other realities,
This is how love is meant to be.

HEART-GUARD

Be not a martyr, for the pains in my life.

Do not deny me, my process of growth,

As you lift me into our now.

You do not over-stand the path or journey,

For this is not for you to do.

Simply hold my heart,

Within the palm of your hands,

As our spiritual travels, leaves it unscarred,

Designed for You, in which to keep it safe...

You are "My Heart Guard."

LOVE IS EVERYTHING

Sometimes we forget and or need a reminder, that

"Love Is Everything!"

We go through our experiences in life and at times
we lose sight of this component.

No matter the outcomes and life's encounters, I
remind myself of this. Because it is a vital necessity
to my existence and to life itself.

It is the link to humanity. Without it we are
inhumane.

Without Love, we have decided to be divided, from
our very existence.

"Love Is Everything" "We Are Love",

"We Are Everything"...

Just "BE!"

WE ARE 1

You think I don't love you,
For all that you've done,
I've done...What we've done to one another,
And all that we've been through.

We've been right, we've been wrong,
Yet we are bonded by our existence.
Forgiveness, over-standing & compassion are the
keys,
To the doors that are locked.

The distanced silence brings no pause,
To the unconditional love, sealed to your creation.
I Love You...
&
We Are 1.

LOVE IS EVERYWHERE

It is in the air, the breeze,

the rustling of leaves,

that reminds us that it exists.

It is in the sun, the sky,

in the hearts of passers-by,

even if we don't see it.

Love is the start,

the beating of the heart,

flowing from realm to realm.

It is a place,

not needing a face,

for all you have to do, is look within.

THE UNIQUENESS OF YOU

Your words, your presence,
Your very essence...
Causes my soul to speak, in a language,
I thought I forgot.

You stimulate my cranium,
Overloading me, in this millennium,
Causing my 3rd-eye,
To see the realness of YOU.

A sense of care,
Wanting and needing you near.
Combining of our energies, into a powerful oneness,

Baffling the Universe, with our ultimate perfected
union...

The uniqueness of you.

DID I TELL YOU?

Did I tell you how much I love you?
Just as much, as the sun shines, bursting forth,
With an energy felt within one's inner core.

Did I tell you that I care?
Regularly, as the stars shine,
Illuminating the path upon which our energetic
connection sustains itself.

Could you perceive, you and I, together?

Just as the riverbank accompanies the waters,
Deep within, combining forceful under-currents,
side-by-side.

Did I tell you, that I'll always be here for you?
Rivaling with Eternity,
Overlapping the embroidered fabric of "time"
A permanent structure, in all realms of existence.
"Did I Tell You?" ...
Now you know.

Inspired by true love's caress.

WE ARE ALL HUMANS

It's been a long, hard and exhausting fight from the
beginning.
Loss of lives, generations, communities,
countries...no one's really winning.

Set in place by those who are forever extracting,
Our very essence, with tactics of distracting.

No love, just hate, taking over the place,
Forgetting, "We Are All Human", sharing this space.

"The Great Divide", all over the world.
We must rise-up, awakening together, forcing the
oppression to unfurl.

Once you were so close...
I swore the earth stood still.
Silenced by the energetic passions, flowing through
my essence.

I parted my lips to speak...
Yet no words were spoken.
Overwhelmed by the closeness of your existence.

Close your eyes...be still.

Conjure my being within your mind,

Drawing me nearer with each thought.
We need not find, what already exists.

One never knows what the future holds.
Living in the now, will lead us on a journey without
end.

We will be close again.

(((BOWING GRACEFULLY)))

Inspired by the response from an individual in life's journey. A consistent reminder, that we are the Keepers of Souls...We are the Lovers of Life, "Namastè & One Love"

LOVE FOUND

Once you were so close...
I swore the earth stood still.
Silenced by the energetic passions, flowing
through my essence.

I parted my lips to speak...
Yet no words were spoken.
Overwhelmed by the closeness of your existence.

Close your eyes...be still.
Conjure my being within your mind,
Drawing me nearer with each thought.

We need not find, what already exists.

One never knows what the future holds.
Living in the now, will lead us on a journey
without end.
We will be close again.

*Inspired by the response from a special individual
in my life's journey.*

THE DANCE

Be still.

As the beating of the drums mirrors the rhythm of
the heartbeats.

Swaying to the energetic tunes, heard only, by those
destined to dance.

Flowing together, like a river in its bank. Pulled like a
magnetic force,

aching for the union of the movements.

Sighs of contentment escape from the pores of our
essence.

Blended in fixated motions,

pausing the very breath of life, perfectly placed by
the meshing of emotions.

Pulsating rapidly, in the same direction, becoming
one, with...

"The Dance."

*Inspired by the rhythmic flow that men & women
have, once they join forces. "DYNAMIC!*

THE FLOW

The flow,
has to go
where it is meant to.

The journey,
is an individual
one to take.

Yet,
it doesn't have to be done
alone.

Feel,
the real deal
within yourself.

YOU

are the path,
and the journey.

Revolve & Change,
right
where you are.

Pushing you,
to move forward
into oneself.

WE LOVE YOU – ODE TO THE "BLACK" MAN

The stillness of your heartbeat,
echoes in my mind.
Memories of lost loves,
lagging sluggishly behind.

Thick as the heat,
burning, from the sun of desires,
I wonder our purpose,
the fuel to our fires.

Inhaling the mist,
as it permeates, from the vapors of his sweat.
The Melaninated coating,
protector of the being tied to the beating in your
chest.

Glistening, sinewy flanks,
bearing the weight not just upon which he stands,
As the gaze of awe, leads to his broad wing-
spanned back,

"We Love You", Our Men of "Black."

*Inspired by the love for our "Black" men.

JUST SMILE

It is there as it crosses the borders of your soul,
A perfect window into the heart that you claim as
your own.
Existing through the trials & tribulations of life,
A reassurance to self and the world,
That no matter the journey, everything will be
alright.
A visual imprint of the embroidery of you,
Through it all, it continues to shine through.
Strong, bright, mighty and blessed,

You share it with others, a perfect release from
stress.
Never let it leave you, for there is no better place to
start,
Than to share such a gift, directly from your heart.
Just smile.

FAMILY

I LOVE MY GRANDCHILDREN

I love my grandchildren.

For when I look, I can see,

Tiny, perfected, reflections of me.

Little hands, feet, and eyes,

The physical essence of love's,

Fundamental surprise.

I could go on forever,

With this delightful poetic note.

Grandchildren are the seedlings of hope.

"I LOVE MY GRANDCHILDREN!"

This I proudly yell.

Grandma, yes Nana, loves you all dearly & always;
Amaya, Promise, LJ, Dynesti, Zashia, & Kendell!

Inspired & dedicated to my Grandchildren.

*THE LITTLE THINGS

As I close my eyes, I feel the gentle caress of a soft
breeze,
I peek at the tree tops, the rustling of leaves.
I can hear children laughing; someone's car
refuses to start,
Dogs are barking for the nearest park.

Car horns are blowing, a bus roars by,
The sunshine bursts throughout the sky.
If you stay still for a moment, wait for the down-
wind,
You can smell all the foods cooking, in various
kitchens.

You can enjoy flush carpets of green grass or fresh
fallen snow,
It is all so positive, whichever way you choose to
go.
I may not have great, monetary things,
But it's the little joys in life that makes it worth
living.
I have learned not to trade them in for anything.

Just look all around, and you will see Earth's
blessings.
Sometimes it's just, *"The Little Things."*

*Published: "The Little Things", by M.A.M. aka Maxine A.
Moncrieffe, Our Times Newspaper, Jamaica, NY, March
2015*

SWEET T

Cool & Brown

Precious to the touch

A look that I love so much

Flowing in a way,

I will always remember

Perfect arrival on a cold day in December

Delicate fragrance

Spectacular to behold

Created from a love, that's never been told...

"Sweet T"

Inspired by my youngest daughter.

I LOVE YOU MOMMY

You carried me in your womb,
protected against all elements.
You brought me forth - Even though you were lost.
You taught me to walk, to talk, to read & to heed...
I learned how to depend on Self, for all of my needs.
Urging me to ALWAYS ask questions,
Oh Mommy, I still do! Over & over again.
You came from Jamaica - Land of Wood & Water,
Precious, oh Precious - Nature's daughter.
When you fell, I fell too but

I overstood your pain. For I too trotted with our
generational strain.
"Once a man, but twice a child",
Even in hospice, lol, I made you smile.
I wrote this poem, especially for you,
Do you remember when I was 5 & wrote my 1st
Haiku?
I used to long for the years of miscommunications &
lost.
But a bouquet of roses you got daily, no matter the
cost.
Yes, I'm grown and some may laugh & think it's
funny,
But I will call you My Baby-Girl, My Mommy...

I Love You Always, may your Soul remain within me.

*I was simply missing my Mom. She was 62 years
young when she transcended due to Cancer (2008).
My Mom was the 1st Poet in my life and my hero. She
suffered from mental illness & put me out of her home
by the time I was 11 years old (Brooklyn, NY was
something back then). We had a turbulent relationship
until one day I realized that my Mom was suffering
from mental illness. I couldn't remain angry at her, no

matter the damage that was done. How can one remain bitter & angry when a person's going through mental hell...For the majority of their lives? I couldn't.

So, I took care of her until she closed her eyes. She was my best friend & my Baby.

Mental Illness is real, and it can & does destroy lives. More people suffer from it than we know, realize or care to acknowledge. Heck, who hasn't lost it here & there, especially when life can batter you from pillar to post? It's important to remember our HUMANITY, LOVE, OVERSTANDING & COMPASSION. Because those that are suffering?...Are our Mothers, Fathers, Siblings, Aunts, Uncles, Cousins, Grandparents, Children, Friends, Wives, Husbands, Pets, and yes, even ourselves.

Rest In Love Mommy.

#Food4Thought

GREAT EXPECTATIONS

It's a girl...maybe,
We can't be sure.
Not in the mood for delivery,
While being pushed through the hospital doors.
"It's a girl!", sounding convinced,
Yes, they laughed as I winced.
Try as they might to determine its sex,
but the baby kept crossing its legs.

Worn & tired, no energy just moans,
I don't want to, it's no big deal, I want to go home.
Then came the words that could not be undone...

"Ma'am, you're going to have a SON."
There was a burst of electricity and gone was the
pain.
A boy! Ha! Haaah! I already chose his name.
Hurry! Get my room ready - for inside me was a
Prince!
Ready to make his grand entrance.

Bearing all pressure, breathing through the strain.
focusing on one thing, rubbing my swollen stomach,
Over & over again...
"The pain is worth it, I'm giving birth to a King!!!"
His father, a piece of him & I reproduced, right there.

I saw no one else, I didn't really care.
I kissed & caressed the crown of his hair, thrilled
that
my great expectation had finally appeared..."My Son."

*"This poem was written and inspired by the
experience of being pregnant and giving birth to my
Son. We didn't know the sex of the baby. I already
had two girls and gave up on getting a boy. It wasn't

until I was in such high risk, that they did an emergency sonogram. Mind you, I was tired, worn, in pain, and had no energy to even move. When they told us that they saw a scrotum? I jumped off the table, did a dance & sang and whined (Jamaican Dancing) all the way to the delivery room, lol! The doctors swore I couldn't have been the same woman who could barely move 25 minutes ago, lol! It was the hardest pregnancy & birth I
             ever had. But I didn't care.

I WAS BIRTHING A SON, A PRINCE, A KING!"
You couldn't tell me anything.
8 & a 1/2 pounds, 23 & 3/4 inches,
                MY SON!"

"Namaste & One Love"

NICHOLE

It was hot, muggy and steamy,
As swollen hands, feet and stomach,
Were being stretched beyond means.

The consistent churning,
Flexing and mighty movements,
Beneath my navel.

18 and scared,
That my baby would be born too late.
Wondering if it would have all fingers & toes.
Would my child look like me?

Would my child look like his/her father?
Would my child even know who I am?
Would my child love me?

I rub my stomach, ever so gently,
Eager to meet the creation,
Reproduced, from deep inside of me.

Flashing of pains, gasps from the strain,
"WuP-WuP- WuP- WuP", the baby heart monitor
pulsates,
Warning me of the contraction, ready to hit!
Big, bright, brown, full twinkling eyes,

Curly black & brown hair,
The cutest little nose,
Skin beyond compare,
Dimpled cheeks, arms and legs...
Attached to a cry that only this mother could feel
and understand.
A lovely life...which is, "You."

Inspired & written for my eldest daughter

SISTERS

When life is so busy keeping us busy, we need a
friend.
Sisters love you, from the beginning to the end.

A true confidant, guide, and shoulder to lean on.
A therapist and even sometimes, even a mother-like
connection.

Or simply that person you can talk to,
Without grudges or spite.

Sisters are great companions, in this journey of life.

We may disagree, some may think that we swerve,

Especially during times, when get on each other's
nerves.

But we are so much more than that. A Sister is life's
proverbial, pat on the back.

They can be biological or not,
as they provide & sustain
a purpose and need, they cannot be forgot...

A symbol of love, and care. A Sister that loves you,
will always be there.
I Love All My Sisters.

Dedicated to my sisters biologically and genetically.

A MOTHER

I wanted to be a Mother,

To children,

Who no longer wanted any parts of me?

Wanting to love my seeds,

The way I never could.

The way in which, my damaged Soul couldn't be.

Lost within the inner struggles of what to do,

The abuse, the hell...

They never really knew

Gone is the yearning
When a Mother is no longer needed.

Erased from the loop of time, no pains from birth, no
sweat or bleeding.

Watching chaotic, lost, & painful dysfunction,

Trapped Souls in their eyes.

Does the pain of a Mother ever die?

MY NATALIE

It's been so long since I've seen you,

Hugged you & shared special moments.

From childhood, adulthood, womanhood, & life.

We share a bond, ever so strong, that even 11 years

Of distance could not break.

We have always shined on opposite sides of the coin.

Yet still, together we are whole.

A light in my life, a Godly blessing, preserved
through time.

Selfishly I claim, created just for me...

I simply love, "My Natalie."

Some cousins can be a rare gem!

FAMILY

Initial views of reactions,

Derived from the strands of DNA,

Linking into one bloodline.

Stamping within,

A sense of pride, love, strength & loyalty.

Forging a path & pattern, to the overall existence of this Universe.

Unrelated genes,

Forming infinite bonds & connections,

Based on experiences together...life...Family.

Inspired by my biological & life-made family.

INNA MI BLOOD!

Mi nuh noe wah ah di problem yuh nuh?
Afftah all, dis yah dayum talkin',
bout seh, mi ah Yankee. Choops!
Tell mi now. A wah all dis yah noise fah?

*KMT!
Yeh, a Foreign mi bawn. Seh wah?
But mi parents dem?
Dem ah natural bawn Yardie!
Most ah my family memba dem? A strictly Yard dem
bawn & grow.

Suh a wah dat mek mi? Ah Jamerican??? Lol!

Nuh true seh America mi bawn.
Nuh watch nuh face!
Jamaica runs trew my veins.

Mommy did ah look opportunity,
an Daddy did ah tek disadvantage!
Ah suh it guh.
Ah nuh my fault dat!

JAMAICA? Chuh-h-h!
No question nuh dideh!
JAMAICA?
It inna mi blood sah!
Heh-Hehhh!

Yah Mon...Yuh dun noe!
Nobody caayn deny mi.
Cause, I and I FEEL di riddim ah my people.

Mi set inna di position, widdout inquisition,

Dat a deh suh, fimmi people come fram.

A deh suh, my Ancestors call out to me &
Mek mi noe seh,
ah dem a help fi carry mi trew. A pon fiddem back mi
tan.

Jamaica? Kmt!
Mon?
It Inna Mi Blood!

"Out of Many, One People"

*KMT (Kiss Mi Teeth)

HEARTACHE

I HAVE A BROKEN HEART

I have a broken heart that needs mending,
the pain is never-ending,
as I am not good at pretending,
that I don't care.
There was something good between us,
but your actions made it a minus,
you did what you wanted, just because,
and now my soul is bare.
I don't know how long it takes to fix it,
I don't think you get it,
you gave my heart stomps &

kicks,
It takes time to heal something so dear.
Your flirting with others is troubling,
you complain about everything,
at times you talk to me like some lost foundling,
as if I'm this dumb thing, that doesn't know what to
do.
I have a broken heart that needs mending,
that you're forever bending, by the ways that make
you, you.
You stated you will never change, my feelings became
rearranged,
and this S.O.S. was caused by you.
See, it's been broken before, that's why I can give you
no

more,
if I continue on, with a love that's forlorn,
There will be nothing left for me. will caress my chest
& do what is best.
I will stay groomed as I lick my wounds,
As life goes on through the mess.
And as I go, only I will know...
I have a broken heart that needs mending.

TRUE COLORS

*"Life is not about waiting for the storm to pass... it's
learning to dance in the rain" ~Anonymous*

You talked, you smiled...knowing all the while,
the mission, in which you set for yourself.
You glided, you moved, fully aware of the grooves,
that only your presence could possibly make.
You laughed, vibed on a whole, showing calmness &
lack of
control, as you exposed the realness, of your lost
Soul.
Putting aside, all that gleamed, expressing what you
really mean,

robbing your essence, your very presence, of who you
are created to be.
I looked out, through the rain, as your Soul begged
to dance again.
But you hardened your ears to the rhythm.
Selling yourself to the highest bidder, not even
leaving, a
minuscule sliver, of the magnificence that once, was
you.
I stand in the rain...all alone, closing my eyes, feeling
my way home..."I Dance!"

I WONDER...?

As I wonder what life has in store for me,
I deal with my fears of inadequacy.
Not sure where it is I'm going,
Wondering if my insecurities are showing.
I think carefully as to what it is I need,
Should I slow down or pick up my speed?
What is it, that I must find?
Where is my thread in this grand design?
Thinking and pondering, what it is I must do,
Saying that I'm worthless...Could this be true?

My heart and my mind are battling, going their
separate ways,
As I wonder, when will something sensible
remain?
Sitting and watching, day-by-day,
As life simply slips further and further away.

As I encounter my thoughts, dreams, and things that
I own,
My fear rises as I travel down the road of the
unknown.
Just trying to put things together and get them done,
Going through the journey, surrounded, yet
alone, wondering about that special one?

Looking at what life has to offer, not sure what I see.
Is this only happening to me?
I wonder...?

Have you ever just wondered about things? Lol, of course, you have! Who doesn't or hasn't? It is a normal action that many living beings have. Many poems have been written in wonder or are the catalyst for wondering to leap from. Wonder can lead to great things.

BUT, YOU DON'T KNOW ME?

You speak with me, every day.
Laying with me, in my private space.
Seeing the expressions, messages relayed,
Clearly displayed upon my face.
Responding with ignorance & a negative tongue,
As you demand to be heard, ALWAYS right NEVER
wrong.
Forgetting the reflective connection, that made us
one.
The binding love, unraveling, becoming undone.

Like a swimmer, drowning & gasping for air,
Arrogance, ego, dance with fear,

Pushing further away, what should be near.
Depleting the bond...In comes the coldness, the land
of no cares,
All that you are, all that you see,
Designed & created...Simplicity.

You fight against self,
As I am the You, that You want to be...
But You Don't Know Me.

*It is amazing how at times when in conflict or at odds
with another, we miss the bigger picture. It starts with
Self. One may want to start with looking at what type
of reflection they're casting. To know others, one must
know themselves.*

HAVE YOU EVER FELT?

Have you ever felt,
So distant & empty
That it seems like it's been centuries,
Since you've been yourself?
Have you ever felt,
That you keep paying the cost,
More stuck than lost,
In a world where you just don't belong?

Have you ever felt,
That as you grow older,
The world seems so much colder,
That you wonder will it remain blind?

Have you ever felt,
That the hand you're dealt,
Must be a lesson,
You simply do not overstand?

Have you ever felt,
That this place is a wild circus,
You've outstretched your purpose,
And it's simply time to move on?
Have you ever felt,
The things that you see,
May never be,
Because Humanity, has lost its love? - Have you ever
felt?

A BROKEN WING

I have a broken wing.
It's hard to see the others, off and flying.

I nurture & caress, my Soul through the stress...
Yearning to be free.

Recalling day & night, the journey, path and flight,
Soon again, to be my own.

A single Soul saw my flickering light.

It stopped to love me through the fight.

Sharing its energy...Even at the risk of being
consumed.
At times, reflecting the fears & doubts that kept me
bound.

Yet...It held on, never letting go.

Sacrificing the "Norm", to help me battle the storms,
outside & within self.
I have a broken wing...That is mending.

Inspired by the thought of a "Knight in Shining Armor.

WHERE IS THE HUMANITY, WHERE IS THE LOVE?

Bustling about, here and there, to-and-fro.
Everyone having somewhere to go.
Heavy hearts, heavier souls,
Losing the energies within self.
Accustomed to the reality of the downtrodden,
Stepping over and past the bodies of the weak
Oblivious and tuned-out,
To the cries of the silent.
Too intertwined with the blindness,
Of ones' own plight and flight in the world of the
materialistic.

Open your soul, open your mind, and open your
heart,
To that place in which love resides.
Remembering that we are Spirits,
Having a Human experience – Human Beings.
Help!
Help Me, Help You, Help We,
Will forever close the gap of heartless ignorance.
"WHERE IS THE HUMANITY, WHERE IS THE
LOVE?"
It is within us all, from the beginning of existence.
Love, Be Love, Give Love, Receive Love.
YOU ARE LOVE!
We can end this needless suffering.

*Inspired by my experience in feeding the homeless
and the hungry in Jamaica, NY.*

I WANTED

I wanted you.
I wanted to feel and to be within you.
I wanted to be the glimmer in your eyes, I wanted
truth.
I wanted to be the friend you never had.
I wanted you to be happy, learning &
to be your rock during the sad.
I wanted to travel with you to wild places.
That cranial trip, through the void & empty spaces,
That makes you, you.
I wanted so much,
It now seems so selfish of me, towards you.

A cluttering of stuff...
I wanted and wanted,
Now it's all daunted because I forgot to find out if you
wanted it too.

Sometimes we forget that relationships are not just about, what you want. It must be a mutual over-standing. So, there must be mutual goals, expectations, and the willingness to compromise. Above all, be open to, and ready for change & to change. Remember, it takes two ☺.

INSPIRATION

"What's more inspiring, than love, life, joy, happiness, positive change, kindness compassion, and forgiveness?" ~Maxwanette

I SHINE
Through this life, connecting and disconnecting,
From the positive & negative...
"I SHINE"
Dealing with the emotions as wide as oceans,
swimming against the undercurrents,
from lack of loves & devotions...
"I SHINE"
Evolving and revolving, learning to be whole &
pulling out of self,
To become in love with the creation that I AM...
"I SHINE"

Letting go of past pains & strains, the blames left at
the wayside,
I rise, content & happy, upon my face is the hugest
smile...
"I SHINE!"

*I felt the need to share this piece. Life is full of
experiences. No matter what the experience and or
encounter is, remember, "WHO YOU ARE & CREATED
TO BE." Own your existence.*

UNIVERSAL OVERSTANDING

"We are there, here, everywhere,
and anywhere.
Limitless and able to create, wherever we go"...

Greater than even the expectations
of self.
Risen from the ashes of destruction,
Filled with the "Knowledge of Self."

Created solely within,
Flooded with the power of the Universe,
Mirroring the reflections of one another.

Melaninated Gatekeepers, awakening...
Forging their rightful places.
Overcoming the distractions, created,
To "Divide & Conquer" HUMANITY.

*"Sacrifice, Responsibility, Healing, Resolve,
Challenges, Unconditional Love"
~33(6)*

"Namaste & One Love"

I REFUSE TO GIVE IN!

The sadness of the day, threatens to not go away,

The negativity doesn't want me to win.

But I refuse to give in. The wind blows so cold,

hearts ache, like bones that are old,

Pain knocks at the door, looking for more victims,

But I refuse to give in. Do not be swayed or feed into the dismay,

negativity also has to find a place within.

I will continue to rise, have love in my heart, soul & eyes...

Because, I, Refuse To Give In!

We all know that life can throw you curveballs, that you simply didn't see coming or weren't prepared for. The point is, "Shit Happens." However, I find the best way to succeed, is to deal with it and don't let the negative defeat you. Instead, acknowledge it, stand up to it, conquer it, & re-channel the energy into something positive, learn from it, master it, and keep it moving.

DO YOU THINK THAT YOU'RE ALONE?

Do you think that you're alone?
As the feelings of isolated desolation,
Leaves you so forlorn.
Barely wanting to move,
Wishing you forgot how to breathe

Whilst dancing on that tight rope of mental disease.
Do you think that you're all alone?
Your tenacity & bravery, that you never notice,
They live past the psychological torture that your
brain thinks this is.

Many may try to degrade your presence,
As they throw their negative 2 cents,
At the breaking of your silence.
Do you think that you're all alone?
The pains that you feel, cause others to deal,
With the pains & struggles, that they're going
through.
Such a precious sacrifice,

Expressing the effects of this life,
And the toll it took... that is how it looks.
Do you think that you are all alone?

Then come, these words of empathy & love are for
you.
And it is okay,
I used to think that I was alone too,
But look? I found you.

*This poem was created out of an empathetic need. I encountered many damaged Souls in this life. Which is easier to do, if you're damaged as well. The beauty is the healing. Along with seeing and knowing of self, loving oneself regardless, basking in this love, saturating in it and sharing it with others. Sharing this love, heals from within and then outwardly. This Universe (World, Earth, Planet) is too big and filled with too many people, for anyone to feel, stay, be, or believe that they're all alone through the madness. No matter how crazy, unfair, painful & defeating it gets, someone is sending positivity your way, someone is trying to remind you that true love exists, someone is encouraging your Soul to remember that love began with YOU, someone is rooting for you to become aware and acknowledge, that you're divinely created, preciously gifted, seriously needed

&

"YOU ARE NOT ALONE."

PUBLISHED

Is there a reason to be published?
Why?...
Because my words need to establish,
their purposeful destination.

There is no simplicity, traveling throughout this
journey.
Yet here I am, still going through the paces,
that relay the spaces of timed things undone.

It is ever so vital,
that my words don't become idle.
As they're falling upon the ears of life,

and felt through searching Souls.

The mission continues, as I trod on
within my purpose.
The Storyteller, Poet, Wordsmith of Prose!
Filled with vocabulary & meaning instead of ego.

I WILL BE PUBLISHED!
By self or through others...Why?
For the road of my destination says so.
Read on.

#WhenYouRefuseToGiveUp

GAINS FROM LOSS

Hurtful feelings plastered on that proverbial wall.
Regrets and sorrows, hoping they would fall.
If we could turn back the hands of time,
Would we cease to exist...at all?

Lost time, missed moments, stuck deep in the past.
The falling rain, disguised tears, that flow ever so
fast.
Strolling through, "The Hall of Memories",
watching life in mirrored frames.

Would of's, should of's, could of's, racking the mind,
laying the blame.
No way to go back, to undo what has already been
done.
Impossible to take away from the zero and adding in
a one.
The point is to embrace the pain, learn from the
mistakes,
and accept the gains.

Stand tall and stay strong, coupled with your rights
and your wrongs.

A wiser & happier person you will remain.

Inspired by mistakes, loss, gains, and life lessons.

ENERGETIC FLOW

It came.
Not with bangs or whimpers,
It simply was, is...here. Always has been.
Stripping away at the core,
That were the ingredients of the metal,
That formed the chains to my existence.
"PHYSICIAN! HEAL THYSELF!"
The declarative statement,
Reflected from my Pineal Gland...
As the energy of my being,
Catapulted its strength,
Through my flesh-bound vessel of transportation.
Feeling the lack of the 3-D gravitational pull,

Created for this Matrix~Illusion,
My footsteps tread, ever so lightly, mirroring the
movements, of nature's rhythm.
The journey & knowledge continues,
Reminding & reconnecting the binary codes of self.
As the views of this life, are still, ever so amazing,

I flow on...

LIFE

It's Beautiful...

An ever-flowing, everlasting, ever-being thing.

As it envelopes my body,

I feel it, so energizing...

"LIFE!"

YOU STAND

Knocked down, beaten, dragged, persecuted,
unfairly judged, taught to self-sabotage.
Giving birth to children on the repetitive cycle,
of the Matrixed Hamster-Wheel.

Lost in the illusions of Heaven,
while living Hell right here on Earth.
Seeking of answers to questions, that you are
reminded,
you already have the solutions to.

Running from others as you run from self,

to come full circle, back to who you are.
"Round & Round you go", Where you stop?
Only you know.

Learning what books only preach,
that only you can teach, how to love thyself.
With "Knowledge of Self" ...
"YOU STAND."

I WISH!

Sometimes, I wish I had a magick wand.

I would change so many things in this world,

starting with myself.

Gone would be pain & suffering,

greed & non-loving, hatred of self and of others.

There would be, no more heartbroken mothers.

I wish I had a magick wand - war, hunger, & famine
would disappear.

There would be no room for sickness,

and death would be a transcended comforting.

We would communicate without words but through
telepathic love.

With smiles and feelings, that everlasting knowing
that we're made of.

I wish I had a magick wand...

"ABRACADABRA!!!"

PHYSICIAN, HEAL THYSELF

I needed healing,
from the feelings,
that had me bound in my own personal hell.

I had to find a calm,
that would caress the storm,
that brewed within my being.

I took this invention called time,
contorted it and make it mine,
in order to remember who, I AM.

Burning my oil & sage,
it silenced the distractions & pain
as the binaural beats connected with my Soul.

Leaving the chaos & background noise behind,
the bright place of quiet light,
welcomes me, as my Chakras realign...

Ahhh, "Physician Heal Thyself!"

IT'S ALL ABOUT YOU

I used to be in a very dark place.
There was zero tolerance & limited space,
For this emotion, that's called love.
I couldn't bear the sound of my own name.
As if mentioning it was to blame,
For the negativity in my existence.

A spiritual flight,
Fighting with all of my might,
I struggled, just because.
Through the hustle & the grind,
With this life, that I claim as mine,
I became distracted from whom I was.

I do not buy into luck,
I refuse to remain stuck,
For I was designed & created to NEVER give up.

When times arrived & I had no clues,
I banged my head on the proverbial wall until it was
black & blue.
I quieted my mind, spoke to my Soul,
And I felt, my way through.

Here I AM, existing,
with the sheer strength of my will,
to make my commands come true.

I will make it, no matter where I am, or what others
do.
Find your strength, magick, power & synergy from
within...
And become the divine creation that is YOU.

LIVE-IT!

Did you take this thing called time?

Draw a line, and measure your existence with it?

Have you conformed, dancing with the norm,

worried & concerned, that your life can be gone
before you begin it?

Do you weep and mourn? As others die and life goes
on,

as you question your place in it?

Does your life take a toll? While you question your
goals,

Pondering life and your purpose within it?

What should I do? Where should I go?

This is my life and how do I fulfill it?

Lol, oh my dear Human Soul, you have forgotten
your role.

Simply Love, be positive, help one another along and
LIVE IT!

FLIGHT OF LIFE

Fluttering around rapidly

Flying into the proverbial walls of life

Still & stagnated moments...

One may even assume, that death has arrived

In ways...death was ever ruling, over millions of times

Recharged & revived, by reconnecting with self

Flapping of wings

"Never giving up--Never giving in"

Constant vibrations & movements

Flutters becoming flaps, flaps becoming flight,

And the freedom, within this Universe, continues...

NOW!

The daze of confusion--

"Bursting forth with Knowledge!"...

Broken and apparent, upon the faces of the masses.

Reality breaking the veil, covering the Pineal Gland.

Forcing it to feel its way open and fully awake.

A deeper over-standing of self, Love and Others,

Joy in the union with the animals, really our friends.

Humanity becoming each other's Keepers,

Moving forward, radiating within the Exodus...

The survivors of this realm. Resonating with
harmonious frequencies

Being at one with the Universe, which is within Self.

The song of the souls, sing...

"Namaste & One Love

THE RHYTHM

I caress, the rhythm of my vibes,

re-shaping & redefining my existence.

Oblivious to the negativity,

that had me stuck,

within the loop of life.

Burning, with the internal fires.

As I rise from the ashes I created.

I forge the continuation,

of Self, past the Pineal views.

Anew, Reenergized, Awoken.

Floating & swaying to the binaural beats,

through the dimensional planes.

I LIVE!

A NEW PLACE

The rustling...

Soothes the Souls,

as Nature & Humanity becomes one.

Red & Gold hues,

gently caress,

the toes of the Sky.

Cemented paths,

guiding and paving,

the journey of its travelers...

And HOME,

becomes a new place,

of adventure.

IS THIS ME?...

Soaring effortlessly

Like a butterfly, free from its cocoon...

Or a rose petal, finally in full bloom

watching the seasons, like a migratory bird

Floating on the Soul of words

Created & designed, from the beginning of time

Is This Me?...

YES!

I ARRIVED

Briefly,

There was a high-pitched squeal.

The kind that makes you stop & feel.

Was it a call?

One that makes, one rethink that,

The very process of freedom is unreachable.

Suckling the breast of existence,

Burping the breath of life.

Continuous are the movements of growth.

Blinking clearly at the resonating of space, time, &
the conceptualization of Self.

Based purely on the rhythmic flow of one's being...

I ARRIVED.

IT JUMPED!

Fluttering, Fluttering, Fluttering,

are the wings, of the caged-bird,

that never sings.

The rhythmic thumping,

Of a restrained heartbeat,

Reminding the body, that it still lives.

Acknowledgment of the damages done.

Worn, broken and torn,

From past storms of flight.

It was now, & at this very moment,

The veiled sight & fears,

Ceased to exist.

Strong, Black, Beady-eyed Bird!

Marking the firmness,

Of things seen, surroundings surveyed.

Naked, featherless body,

Hardened beak & pointedly poised feet,

There it is! That minuscule tingle of movement.

Ignoring of sustenance,

As a planned escape,

Was now INEVITABLE!

Sweat released, creating supple smoothness,

For slippage through the bars,

This was no mere coincidence.

Through an opened window,

Yet, there were no other options,

How to fly.

Contemplating the distance,

Upon the fall,

That was so obvious & apparent,

The bird that was caged,

Glimpsed the safety, of its former stage...

"IT JUMPED!"

DO YOU

Do you see the heart within,
under this skin?
Yes, there's a heart that's beatin.'
Can you look past,
the hateful, negative, & inhumane prisms,
that many are bound to? Trapped with distorted
visuals of life?

Or do you ignore the view,
thinking, it doesn't fit you?... Remember,
we all help create the world, that we live in.
Could you look through the darkness spewed?

So engorged, severely swollen & polluted,
by the things that we do, mucked-up from what
already was, is?

As we are the reflections of Humanity,
yeah, that's right, Me & You...You & Me.
Take heed to the World in which we're creating'
Can we share a little more love,
care, concern, & overstanding?
We can support one another, results in less suffering'
Through this Journey called Life, Flow as One

Come on! Naturally created, Universal Lovers, Coded
beings of hues.
DO YOU!

SOMETIMES YOU HAVE TO STOP...

Sometimes you have to stop......
In order to begin again.

Take a personal inventory,
of your own existence.

Peel away the layers of pain,
And love your being, restore your worth.

Ignoring the madness, that fed the sadness,
That you accepted as your reflection.

Taking away the titles, labels & shackles,

Holding you prisoner, in a jail without walls.

Viewing yourself & this Universe,
As a playground for your soul.

Learning as one goes along,
The story is yours to be told.

Because, sometimes you have to stop,
In order to begin again.

Inspired by Life.

NEW BEGINNINGS

As the old fades into the background,

The path to self,

Is grounded in my mind's eye.

No longer shackled to the drudgery, of the
condemned.

Instead, I take a fresh breath,

As life continues.

One of three, I stand forward,

In front of the line,

Of my own experiences.

Around the proverbial bend, I move on again,

Onto the infinite journey, that has no end...

Starting of, "New Beginnings."

Inspired by beautiful experiences. ~Mississippi 2016.

OPEN YOUR EYES!

Open your eyes! Don't you recognize me?
Do I not calm your fears & dry your tears?
Am I not the ear that is open,
when your mouth runneth over with grief?
Is it not my bosom you cling to for comfort?

It is US, who accepts YOU as you are.
For to us, you are a being of great things,
presently & to come.
We see the wonderfulness of you.

Behind those dark & moody eyes, troubled heart &
mind?
Is a man, better than all men...A KING!
You capture our hearts,
but so many times, you foolishly break them &
cast them aside.
For you do not see, nor do you overstand the rare
gift bestowed upon you.

You are the crowns & we are the jewels that
bringeth forth your glories. Fixated & cemented
within your being. To be held high above your head
& cherished...But alas, you have forgotten Self &
your Queens.

With our hearts, we give you all the love, that one
can give, without losing our life's essence.
We love you, with every fiber of our beings.

We are loyal, trustworthy, & can make the sun
jealous with the brightness of our smiles of love
towards you.

Perfection we may not be. Rusty around the edges? Maybe.
But pick us up and dust us off, guarding, sustaining, protecting, maintaining, and loving us, & we shine brighter than any diamond.
We are the rarest of treasures, sought by many, far and wide,

yet, we are yours and cling to the magnetism of melanin.
And all that we are, are the loving reflections of you.
OPEN YOUR EYES!

*Inspired by the love and connection felt towards our Brothers, Men...Our "KINGS." Despite having been hurt by many of them, the majority of my life, watching the pain they inflicted and inflict, on other Sister~Queens, their seeds, family, others, and even themselves, witnessing this place stripping them from a sense of self and purpose, tearing them down in our eyes and in the eyes of the world, until they become masters of their own destruction...
I still LOVE OUR "BLACK" KINGS. I simply am no longer a container that harbors the negative ones. However, I overstand why, they are, the way that they are (our Sister~Queens as well). "WE ARE, WHO WE ARE." The key, is to gain "KNOWLEDGE OF SELF", "Feel, Deal, Heal & Keep It Moving Forward"...TOGETHER.*

CREATIVITY

"Creativity Is Humanity's (Humanities) Algorthim"
~Maxwanette

LUVIN' DI BOB!

Listening to you daily, in my youth,
You became a mentor, friend, a vision of truth.
Sneaking to play your music, under the covers in
bed,
As your words & sounds were imprinted within my
head.
Wishing that you didn't physically die,
As it was you, who first helped to re-open, my 3rd-
eye.
A legend, a master, out doing time,

I sing & hum your chunes, line-by-line.
Many have gone & many will come,
But you're a lyrical prophet & can never be matched
or undone.
Grown, that I am, yet these ears & eyes still see,
There will never be another like, "Robert Nesta
Marley."
"One~Love."

*Inspired by my #1 & favorite artist & teacher, during
my childhood, "Robert Nesta Marley aka "Bob
Marley." Like many, I grew up rather rough and
underprivileged. Through the pain, and confusion felt
that I endured as a child...I needed answers. I grew
up listening to Bob Marley and by the age of 8, I
knew a great deal of his music by heart. My mother
didn't allow "Dat Rasta Mon Music," to be played. I
was taught that Rastafarians were evil, of the devil,
murderers, rapists, nasty, foul, dirty, and
ignorant...Similar to the fictional description of a
"Troll." My mother HATED anything with locs. Passed
along through the family – that's a story for another
book, lol! But Bob? He taught me about life and made
me want to seek more answers. He also opened my
mind up to the world in which we live in. I would sing*

his songs and cry. At times, I swore he was singing about and for me...Singing to me. Then I began to see, that he was. He was singing for all that could relate & or over-stand the meaning of his lyrical visions & life. I don't miss him, because for me? He lives on forever. His words & messages are timeless. He will never die. Respect & One Love Brother Bob.

SILENCE

In a space of total love & acceptance,

feeling the vibrations of my very existence.

The quietness of who I Am,

refocusing on the connection,

I have with self.

Releasing the imbalance,

and realigning, to the shift within...

Finding my place, deep inside...the "Silence."

It is within these moments of silence, that I am most creative, loving and extra over-standing with self. I embrace who I am in a cocoon-type fashion.

PUBLISHED

Is there a reason to be published?
Why?...
Because my words need to establish,
their purposeful destination.

There is no simplicity, in traveling throughout this
journey.
Yet here I am, still going through the paces,
that relays the spaces of timed things undone.

It is ever so vital,
that my words don't become idle.
As they're falling upon the ears of life,

and felt through searching Souls.

The mission continues, as I trod on
within my purpose.
The Storyteller, Poet, Wordsmith of Prose!
Filled with vocabulary & meaning instead of ego.

I WILL BE PUBLISHED!
By self or through others...Why?
For the road of my destination says so.
Read on.

#WhenYouRefuseToGiveUp

DO DAT TING!

Do dat ting!
That makes me swing,
To the rhythmic beats, of your vocalist creations.

Damn, if I don't jam,
To the sounds of your flow,
That go, deep within my soul.

Mi tamp mi feet,
To a dance, oh so sweet,
The grand riddim designed, with our culture &
people in mind...

"Respect - Mr. Tarrus Riley!"

*Inspired & dedicated to the famous and popular
Reggae singer Tarrus Riley.*

THE ARTIST

Existing in this world that at times, seems so cold,
Taking on the task to decipher the DNA of self.

Sketched into the very fabric of every human
being,
Trying to elucidate ones embroidered path.

Wondering if possibilities rely on its unraveling,
Stitch-by-Stitch, breath-by-breath, acknowledging
the beginning.

No longer awed by the destiny of death,

As recognition of the bumps and swirls, once
evaded, now deeply embedded,
In life's mystical yet chaotic blend.

YOU are "The Artist!"
Take up your brush and start, all over again.

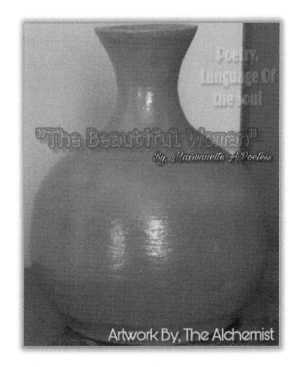

Artwork By, The Alchemist

THE BEAUTIFUL WOMAN

Bare, cool and lucidly naked.
A melded blend of emotional hues,
exposing her prominent figure.
She stands firmly, strongly, uniquely,

powerfully and sleekly composed...

Reflective not of what's contained within.

Well-rounded by her existence.
She knows her purpose,

resulting in her comfort.

A beaconed teardrop in this ocean of life.

Sm-o-o-o-o-th to the touch,

feeding the Soul.
The hunger has been fed,
the Yin & Yang will remain, the appetites of energy.
I am inspired.

*Inspired by & written for the beautiful artwork
created by, Reiki Sculptor: "The Alchemist" aka Jay
Jasper

PRINCE

"This is what it sounds like, When Doves Cry"...a
silent emptiness,
as the "Purple Rain" pummels the earth
I recalled when you said,
"Let's Go Crazy", you "Sexy Motherfucker!",

Because, "U Got the Look", "To Do Me Baby."
"If I Were Your Girlfriend", you'd "Stare",
soon to be "Facedown", wrapped up in my "Pussy
Control."

Becoming my "Hardrock-lover", as "I Feel For You."

As we, "Fallinlove2nite", gently the sunrises,
I don't want any "Starfish & Coffee", for "Breakfast
Can Wait."
"Let's Pretend We're Married." We could just,
"Partyman",
as you do the, "Bat-Dance", that makes me sooo
"Soft and Wet",
in the backseat of your, "Little Red Corvette."

Days have passed..."How Come You Don't Call
Me?"

I love you, "I Hate U" as I am dialing..."777-9311."
You left me? I never knew. Like, "Thieves in the
Temple."
"Every day is a Winding Day"...

You're gone, "This Is What It Sounds Like, When
Doves Cry",

"While My Guitar Gently Weeps."

Inspired by the transcending of Prince
{04/21/2016}

LIVITY

"Life is the 1st precious thing, next to love."
~ Maxwanette

I AM (II)

It took some time, for me to leave behind,

the shackles that bound me.

I was taught to look above, for the reality of Love,

and only it could set me free.

Tearing down the walls, watching the debris of my
life fall, I rise, a renewed being.

Dismantling the deceptions & the lies,

facing truths --- allowing my Soul to cry.

Healing, feeling & knowing,

I AM ENERGY & I WILL NEVER DIE!

The Pineal view of this life shines. We are to be
reminders of Love, rediscovery of self...

"I AM!"

EXODUS LIVING

Are you ready?
Step by proverbial step
YOU are the captain of your own ship.
If the path isn't to your suiting?
YOU are in control.
Baby, Change It!

If the sun forgot to shine,

In your world today?
Then "Dammit!"
Get up and make it!

You cannot change what already has been done,

But YOU are the one, that governs your outcome,

Of how your existence will be.

Wake-up and see, by facing the negative & positive,
You will create how YOU live.
Come on my love...
"Be Free."

RIDING HIGH

I stood, on the hood,

of the car, as it drove through hell.

Viewing the snapshots, of existence,

I blazed on.

Forgiving others & self, for the glitches,

that short-circuited our actions.

Flowing to the humming,

that's in sync, with the binaural rhythm,

Of my heartbeat...

"I'M ALIVE!"

THE TREE

The tree that died, had forgotten how to bloom.

The tree that died, had an empty womb.

The tree that died, lived in a world with no room.

It grew weary, withering & gray.

It was tired, lacking sun, day-by-by.

It sat, it creaked, it bent and waited to fade away.

The tree that died, had deep & strong roots.

The tree that died, wailed & mourned for its fruits.
The tree that died, had given up its pursuits.

It decided that life wasn't worth living.

It decided, it had nothing more worth giving.

It one day just ceased...Still, was it no longer living?

The tree that died, suddenly felt warm.

The tree that died, regained strength through the
storm.

The tree that died, was no longer wronged.
It stood firm, tall, strong...It thrived. It stretched,
grew leaves & fruits in massive size. It reveled in the
love of many lifetimes...

The tree that died? Lol, it came ALIVE!

NATURES SYMPHONY

As the rain showers down,

the coolness of its breeze,

carefully yet gently soothes,

before the roared, bang of thunder, warns of its deep
intentions.

Through brief intervals,

the birds chirp wildly,

as if to warn each other to stay put,

for more is yet to come.

The silence within the noise,

Blends & produces...

The beauty of Nature's Symphony.

CLEANING-UP

See, I had some cleaning-up to do today,
I had a whole bunch of clutter,
busy getting in my way.
As I took to the task, with no one to ask,
I stepped into the maze of my life,

I did some cleaning-up today.
I opened sealed boxes, used what was good,
lifted & inspected everything I had under the hood.
No more burdens, stresses, and strains.

No more outrunning myself and pressuring my
brain.

Unlike or like some, I came from a poor, lost, ill-
fated sect.
Born was I, with feet on my neck.
Used & abused, silenced in so many ways,
Gone was my innocence, never a game to be
played.
Taught no value of my body, soul, and head,
A child, oh so young, yet the living dead.

I no longer look at the loss,
The sacrifices, the cost.

Now I laugh, and find the joys in things,
Oh, so appreciative of my mentally projected
blessings.

Cause see, I had some
cleaning-up to do today.
I had to go through the labyrinth of my life, to find
my way.

Life will have tears, pains, disappointments ahead,
But once you have life, you are not dead.

I got down & dirty, stepped deep in the grease,
I rose; clean, grounded and realized I needed more
than just peace.
So, I did some cleaning-up today, I found a way to
be set free.

I did some cleaning-up today.
The cleaning within Me.

*Cleaning from within, allows for a clearer path in
life.*

*Published: 2014, Domestic Violence Aftermath – By,
Broken Publications, "Cleaning-Up" Pg. 160.*

KUJICHAGULIA! (SELF-DETERMINATION)

I am an unstoppable force of nature and the Universe,

embodied in this fleshy covering.

Perfection & Imperfection in a vessel,

that seeks constant & consistent balance.

Justified, Personified, Electrified by the movements of self.

I was, I am, I forever will be,

Embracing the God within Me.
With the Knowledge of Self and the strength of my ancestors,

I will revel in the shifts and changes,

that propels me further, upwards, and onwards.

Fulfilling my purpose as I guide my soul,

in the purpose of helping others & not just for merely existing.

The roar upon the lips of my internal voice, as the Warrior within cries...

"KUJICHAGULIA-A-A-A!!!"

This started out a as a simple post. As my vibes flowed, this poem came to be. Existing in my soul, but now here to be seen. Doing exactly what I am determined to do in getting my poetry out there, my book completed and published. I have learned how to embrace the fire within self and use it to my best

capacities...which are INFINITE, lol! Loving the God in Me.

BUS RIDE IN QUEENS

"Beep-Beep!", "Beep-Beep!",
Go the horns of the Dollar-Cabs,
Tempting one not to wait on transit.

"NOT IN SERVICE" – plastered on the front,
Of bus number 3 as it passes one by,
Shivering in the cold.

Inching casually to the front of the line,
Trying to ignore the evil-eyes that are watching,

Making sure you do not pass them first.

Huddled in the metal & plastic can,
Longing for ones stop to be next.
A tap on ones shoulder...

"Would you like a seat?"
Glad that humanity is not dead.
Oh, what a ride!

Inspired by an experience in Jamaica Queens, NY

MY SISTER~QUEENS

Wake-up, "My Sister~Queens",
and regain, "Knowledge of Self."
We must fix this universe.
Re-strengthening ourselves, dismantling the curse.
.

With assorted crowns,
we are the creators of ALL nations.
It is time for us to know our worth.
We are the life-bringers. We maintain & bring forth,
through birth.

Time to step aside from the madness,

invented for our destructive sadness,
and embrace one another.
Building, Bonding, Loving, Unifying; joining to bring
forth & promote progress.

Do not believe the lies,
as we have been torn down in the eyes,
of the world and all of humanity?
Forgetting who we are, as we wage a war, against self
and our Sistrens.

"Black" Womb-Man!
Chakratic existence, intertwining combination,
the source and force that can defeat

"The Powers That Be."

I am your keeper, "My Sister~Queen",
and you are mine. Standing at the forefront,
at attention and in line.
We have a mission to fulfill.

Listen to your Soul. The message is in the wind.

We can conquer the negativity together,
forever blending, My Sister~Queens of Melanin.

Side-by-Side,
helping our children & our Kings.

Onward through the Exodus from this Matrix...
Together, WE RISE! No stronger has been seen.
It's time for us to remember who we are and embrace
our Sister~Queens.

"Namaste & One Love"

*As "Black" women, it is imperative for us to know,
see, value, and accept who we are and our own self-
worth. In turn, seeing this in our fellow Sister-Queens,
and teaching it to our young. Lifting one another up,
instead of tearing one another down, stopping the
jealousy & the hatred, but instead, holding and
guiding each other, our people, and humanity through
the Universe.*

SEEK ANSWERS

Seek answers from WITHIN.
No one can do it like YOU.
Who else should be in charge of YOU but YOU?

THINK, ACT, MAKE IT BE---

POWER is within each and every one of us.
There are NO limits except if you create or believe
in them.
Create your own positivity. Control YOU. And
connections will be limitless.

Eliminating the negativity of dual falsehoods, as
you lift the veil from your 3rd-Eye.

It will resonate like a multitude of magnetic waves,
across the world, lacking only in timelessness...
Now what is more powerful than that?

DESERT ROSE

Standing firmly, straightforward, and correct.

No harm may come to you, for you are the Chosen
Select.

Beaten, ravaged, and revived by your
surroundings,

with a blooming grace so immense, so astounding.

Delicate soldiers with posture & purity,

as the world gazes upon your definitive beauty.

Left to your solitude in a place so bold & dry.

You lift your beautiful head as if to kiss the sky.

Deflecting the awed rarity of your existence, while

barraged by the elements of life's circumstances.

Surrounded by the predators yet engulfed with
determination to be.

So regal, so strong, with the ability to exude such
color and odiferousness.

Amidst the monolithic adversities, leaning
mercilessly upon your svelte stem. You are a, Desert
Rose.

Poetry, Language Of The Soul, Vol. I.

DIVINE CREATIONS

"Peace...Bless Up, Grand Rising Kings & Queens!"

A daily quote, that remains the same.

A consistent & conscious reminder,

that we, **#CannotBeContained**!

Melaninated, Avatar-Locs, Strong, Loving Beings.

Ebony-Energies, Elevated, Soulful,

Knowledgeable created energies.

Grateful for your existence,
as you fulfill your divine purpose.

"Weed The People – Cannot Be Contained!"

The Mantra I hum, as I light my sage incense.

*Inspired by King & Queen, Raheen Dodd & Angela Marni Dodd, creators & owners of their own *clothing & accessories line, Constant reminders of the "Power Within!" *Website: https://www.bigdoddscustom.com/*

WORLD OF A POET

The flow of my pen,
over & over again.
The Soul spills its ink.

Feeling the power,
that can devour,
the path taken, to be here.

Revel in the words,
marinated in nouns, adjectives and verbs,
revealing the thoughts within.

Readers need not beware,
shed your doubts and or cares,
It's okay to let the vibes sink in.

"Welcome, to the world of a poet."

RESOURCES

https://www.rainn.org/about-national-sexual-assault-telephone-hotline

National Alliance on Mental Illness

NAMI, the National Alliance on Mental Illness, is the nation's largest grassroots mental health organization dedicated to building better lives for the millions of Americans affected by mental illness.

Helping Those In Need

NAMI started as a small group of families

Call the NAMI Helpline at 800-950-6264 M-F, 10 am – 6 pm, ET
Or in a crisis, text "NAMI" to 741741 for 24/7, confidential, free crisis counseling

Let's talk!

972-357-6387

ZEN-COUNSELING

4425 Plano Parkway Ste 701 Carrollton TX 75010

Offering Saturday Appointments & Telehealth

https://www.zen-counseling.com/

MAXWANETTE'S LINKS:

Stay Connected With Maxwanette A Poetess Please Visit:
FaceBook/Meta:
Maxwanette A Poetess

P.L.O.T.S.~ The Creatives Magazine
https://www.facebook.com/plotsthecreativesmaga zine

Facebook Group: P.L.O.T.S ~ The Creatives Bridge

(1) {P.L.O.T.S.} ~ CREATIVES BRIDGE (formerly the Poetic-Chain) | Facebook

Instagram
https://www.instagram.com/maxwanette_a_poetess

YouTube
https://www.youtube.com/channel/UCQH9Ihu38P7VsE -3ABm6mPA

Get Your Own Chatbook At A Discount!

Chatbooks:
http://invite.chatbooks.com/maxwanetteapoetess5x y

ACKNOWLEDGEMENTS

To my Social Media Family – (WordPress, Facebook, Instagram, Twitter, & YouTube), to My Poetic Family - Brother~Kings & Sister~Queens; Radio host Sister Francine Chin – who referred me to Brother Yasus Afari, who sent me, to Sister Antonia Valaire (aka Christena Williams) – who encouraged me to write my book of poetry, not knowing they were alreadyready for print, lol, Brother Richie Innocent – for accepting me into the poetry family, and words of encouragement, Brother Bob McNeil – for always being a great support and mentor, Sister Timi Oki – wonderful supporter, Brother's Howardmc Hendriks/Tun-It-Up Radio/109Jamz/Ras Manga – for the airtime & promoting my works, Brother Ras Igel - IMW Igel Muzik Wurx – for the wonderful job done on my videos & for inspiring me to find my voice & learning to love it when I heard it, and to "Our Times" Newspaper – Jamaica, NY, ~ for publishing my piece "The Little Things."

DISCLAIMER

Please note, that the author is not a physician, nor psychiatrist. She does not offer resources as a treatment. They are shared for informational use. She does not endorse nor is she employed by any of the resources listed and does not gain any form of compensation. It is always best to check with your doctor, for the treatments that are best suited for you. Don't be afraid to seek help if needed.

MAXWANETTE'S MOTTO'S

"Stay Focused & Ignore The Background Noise."

"We're All In This Thing Called Life, TOGETHER...Remember? Namastè & One Love"

DEDICATED MENTION [2024]

Honored love and respect to my dear, dear friend, and the editor of this book. William Tyrone Murphy, who transcended 05/18/2021, 1 year after we worked on this book. Thank you, Tyrone, for always looking out, and for blessing me, even after you left this world. I will always love you. Rest In Love Ty-Ty. Till we meet again."

Poetry, Language Of The Soul, Vol. I.

{P.L.O.T.S.}~PROOFING & PROMOTING SERVICES, LLC
Ulster County – Kingston, NY 12401
[U.S.A.]

NOTES:

NOTES:

Made in the USA
Columbia, SC
16 September 2024